HOW TO LOVE YOURSELF AFTER BULLYING AND ABUSE

LUCY RUTH

 Created with Vellum

CONTENTS

SUMMARY

DEBUNK AND DEVELOP YOUR MIND. This step-by-step guide to positive thinking and mind detox is designed to help everyone, young and old, to focus and heal from past verbal abuse. Verbal abuse happens at school, work and home. Words are weapons that are used everyday to destroy one's spirit. Often one ends up hearing the bad words repeated by the brain's memory database. The mind, with proper training, can signal good words back into our adrenaline and eventually overcome the bad words. A wise man once told me that evil will never win and the good will always outweigh the bad.

What does Debunk mean?

There are many ways the word "Debunk" can be used in the English language:

- To investigate and prove something is false or true
- To discredit

We are going to use "Debunk" in order to expose the myths or belief systems that we have been programmed to believe or discredit some of the echoing words we have been told by those close to us. We are going to let go of society's negative voices in our minds. These words have scarred our hearts and made us who we are today. In this lesson, we are going to learn to love ourselves back and regain our confidence. We are detoxing all the negativity seeded in us. When a lawn is filled with dandelions, we tend to not see the beauty of our nice green lawns. We are going to uproot the dandelions of bad words embedded in our brains, and we are going to reseed, regrow and repurpose our minds.

We are going to discredit the words that are often said by society - abusive words we hear everyday and everywhere. Below is a list of commonly used bad words that negatively affect people, cause them to feel bad about themselves and leave emotional scars. We are going to debunk them and detoxing our minds because negativity has no place in our beings.

In the spaces provided, write a list of all the positive things you can think of. Create the YOU you want, not what someone else wants.

. . .

The end result of this course is for you to fall in love with yourself and claim victory over negative thoughts.

BULLYING AND DEPRESSION

BULLYING **a major cause in some types of depression**

The rise in bullying in today's world is a trigger to many people who struggle with rejection. Social media abuse, such as bullying, has left some families depressed as a result of their teenagers committing suicide due to bullying. Social media bullying plays an important role in triggering those who are predicted to have a higher level of depressive mood.

Society needs to be aware that some people who might have had bad childhood experiences are prone to depression, according to research. Childhood trauma can induce stress, creating a greater risk of adulthood depression and stressful life events as an adult.

DETOXING your mind plays a fundamental role in addressing post-traumatic depression. With the right tools like meditation and a step-by-step guide to positive thinking, those dealing with the effects of past trauma and verbal abuse can find healing. Unfortunately, the reality is that verbal abuse occurs in places that should be a haven, like school, work and home. When this happens, the words stick and replay in the mind of the victim over and over again. With proper training, however, the brain can overcome the bad words.

Start saying positive affirmations about yourself everyday. FORGET WHAT WAS SAID!

LET GO AND LEARN TO LOVE YOURSELF

WE ARE GOING to do an exercise and use the most common words used by bullies or words commonly used in verbal abuse situations. We are going to replace "Why ME" with "**I AM.**"

Why **ME**?

You have probably asked yourself this question many times. According to research, bullies have a low self-esteem and they feel better about themselves when they bully others. We also have to keep in mind that some bully because they were victims of bullying, too.

1. **"You are Ugly"** - Now this is false. There's no one who is ugly. We are different and we beautify our world with those differences. Repeat to yourself: "**I AM** me and I

love myself. **I AM** beautiful and I add beauty to this world."

Write more positive thoughts in the spaces provided.

____

____

____

____

2. "You are a Bad Parent" - You are the best and don't ever allow your in-laws, outlaws or anyone else ever make you believe you aren't**.** Say **"I AM** a good parent" and write down all the good things and memories you have enjoyed with your children. Reminisce about the good times and laugh out loud or smile. Release good endorphins. You have more space to write and enjoy every moment of it.

____

____

. . .

____

____

3. **"You are an Idiot"** - No, you are a genius. Say "**I AM** a genius with a brilliant mind."

____

____

____

____

4. **"You're a Weirdo"** - You are too intelligent to join foolishness. Say **"I AM** brilliant and I observe and respond where my responses are needed. **I AM** smart and blessed. I do not affiliate myself where it doesn't suit." Embrace your weird heart and love it with all you have.

____

.   .   .

____

____

____

5. **"You are a Bitch"** - You are fearfully and wonderfully made. Say **"I AM** a delightful person with a different approach to circumstances. **I AM** loved my those close to me."

(Write down the good things you have done for others and be proud of it.)

____

____

____

____

6. **"You are FAT"** (I detest this word) - What matters in life every breath that each and everyone one of us breathes. Weight can be lost and a stinky attitude stinks. Repeat these

words if you have ever been a victim of this bad word. **"I AM** a different flower that makes my world a beautiful one. I embrace me. My weight does not define me."

----

7. "**Why don't you go hang?**" **-** When someone says this, never ever take it seriously. That person needs help themselves as they are dealing with their own demons. These words should be erased from your mind immediately. Say to yourself, **"I AM** never going to allow anyone to bully me. **I AM** going to live the best life."

Write down a list of things worth living for. What are your thankful for? If you know the bully, what is missing in their lives? You are worth more and there's no one in the whole world worth dying for. Let go of suicidal thoughts. Take up a new hobby and a new challenge. You will feel more accomplished when you set goals and achieve them. Your achievements are worth every part of you.

. . .

CHOOSE HAPPINESS and exercise mind detox every-day. Use the power of positive affirmations everyday until they sink in your brain. Happiness is an inside job and it must start with you. Declutter your mind by planting posi-tive words in yourself. Put yourself first and foremost. Write a list of things that make you happy and how best can you achieve them. For example, you can set aside thirty minutes for self-care like exercising, doing a daily beauty routine, watching comedy or just relaxing.

Let go of toxic people. Don't ask for advice or share your excitements with negative people as negativity poisons your mind. Write a list of who they are and remind yourself the reasons why you cannot share anything with them.

Start a new hobby. Find something interesting to do; perhaps write your own book. Play a new sport. List a few sports or hobbies you are interested in and find a local club to join.

. . .

Chase your dreams. If you have a dream go pursue it and if at first you don't succeed, try and try again. Write your dreams and how you can achieve them.

Don't dwell on the past. Think about a positive future. When negativity knocks on your brain remind it that its time expired and it is no longer welcome in the new you.What did your experiences teach you? Forget the pain negative people caused but invest in your emotional wellbeing. If you need counselling, talk to your doctor and they will recommend some counsellors in your area.

Think positive even when you are having a bad day. Talk to a close friend or family member. Stay active and occupied. Give yourself time to heal and remember almost everyone carries a hidden scar.

Depending on your situation, sometimes travelling might be a good idea. There are so many beautiful places in every country. Save money and make a habit of taking time away. Get out more and connect with nature.

I love outdoor life. It brings so much peace. In good weather, I like to walk on trails. Just looking at this picture gives me a sense of adventure and leisure. Fall in love with your local trails. Start your own nature collection and discover the beauty around you.

How about getting to know more about the world? Write it down on your list of things to do and work towards saving money to take a trip to a tropical country. How about a Safari trip to Africa with family or friends? I took my kids on a trip of a lifetime to Zimbabwe and they had the opportunity to encounter elephants. How cool is that? There is so much to live for. The world is an amazing place. Talk to your travel agent about a Safari trip to a country of your choice, or alternatively, you can email me and I will be able to help your dream come true. With positive thoughts and having something to look forward to, you will win. Tell yourself life is good and remind yourself about nature.

This is Victoria Falls, Zimbabwe. There's a rainbow at the end of the storm! You survived bullying/verbal abuse. Your new life starts now. Raise your head high. You are loved! Keep hope alive.

This picture makes me laugh. What was this monkey thinking ? I caught it unaware. Now what positive thing can you learn from this? In my opinion, I see a monkey resting and not caring about what's going on around it. Develop the same attitude. Ignore the negative disruptive voices around you. When you do that, you will find peace.

Mr Crocodile is taking a nap. Take time to rest and your mind will thank you for it. Is your mind thinking about vacation now? Well that's the point. Mind detox is a great way to start afresh. When's your next vacation? Write a list of places to visit in the next 12 months.

____

____

____

Isn't the world amazing? Reconnect with Mother Nature. This is part of Victoria Falls which is one of the seven wonders of the world. When I visited this place, I just stood there admiring the beauty. How many wonders of the world do you know? Research them and write your findings. There's power in positivity. Happy researching!

This place is in Hamilton, Canada. It's a must-see place to visit in the summer in hot humid weather. The more we get out and connect the more we heal. With lots of activities and having more time outdoors, we can find peace within our souls. Reconnect with nature.

As I conclude this, I recommend you make a daily habit of telling yourself how special you are. Speak positive words to you mind. Choose a few words from each letter of the Positive Alphabet. Detoxify!

A to Z of positive words.

A

    I AM ADORABLE!
    I AM ATTRACTIVE
    I AM AMAZING
    I AM ALIVE

B

    I AM BLESSED
    I AM BEAUTIFUL
    I AM THE BRILLIANT
    I AM THE BEST
    I AM BRAVE

. . .

C

I AM COURAGEOUS
I AM CHEERFUL
I AM CLEVER
I AM CONFIDENT

D

I AM DESIRABLE
I AM DYNAMIC
I AM DESIRABLE
I AM DELIGHTFUL

E

I AM ENERGETIC
I AM EXCELLENT
I AM ELEGANT
I AM ENCOURAGED

F

I AM FABULOUS
I AM FANTASTIC
I AM FRIENDLY
I AM FUN

G

I AM GENUINE
I AM GREAT

I AM GOLDEN
I AM GOOD HEARTED

H

I AM HEALTHY
I AM HAPPY
I AM HOPEFUL
I AM HUMAN

I

I AM INDEPENDENT
I AM IMPRESSIVE
I AM INCREDIBLE
I AM IRREPLACEABLE
I AM JOYFUL

J

I AM JUBILANT
I AM JOVIAL
I AM JUSTIFIED

K

I AM KIND
I AM KNOWLEDGEABLE
I AM KING

. . .

L

I AM LOVED
I AM LOVING
I AM LOYAL
I AM LIKED

M

I AM MOTIVATED
I AM MARVELOUS
I AM MAGNIFICENT
I AM MERCIFUL

N

I AM NICE
I AM NOBLE
I AM NOTABLE
I AM NEEDED

O

I AM OPTIMISTIC
I AM ORIENTED
I AM OUTSTANDING
I AM AN OVERCOMER

P

I AM PASSIONATE
I AM POWERFUL
I AM PEACEFUL

I AM POSITIVE

Q
I AM QUAINT
I AM QUALITY
I AM QUINTESSENCE
I AM QUEEN

R
I AM REFRESHED
I AM REJUVENATED
I AM REPUTABLE
I AM RESILIENT

S
I AM SENTIMENT
I AM SPECIAL
I AM SMART
I AM STRONG

T
I AM THANKFUL
I AM TRUSTWORTHY
I AM TREMENDOUS
I AM TRANSFORMING

U

I AM UNDER CONTROL
I AM UNDERSTANDING
I AM UNIQUE
I AM USEFUL

V

I AM VICTORIOUS
I AM VALUED
I AM V.I.P
I AM VIBRANT

W

I AM WELL
I AM A WINNER
I AM WORTHY
I AM WONDERFUL

X

I AM XOXO

Y

I AM YOURS
I AM YEARNING FOR MORE OF ME

Z

I AM ZEALOUS FOR CHANGE

. . .

You did it! How did this exercise feel? Feel free to write your testimonies via email at debunkdevelop@gmail.com

YOU ARE LOVED! YOU ARE NEVER ALONE. STAY HEALTHY AND LUCY RUTH WISHES YOU A HAPPY SUCCESSFUL LIFE FILLED WITH POSITIVE OUTCOMES!

NOTES

- -

- -

- -

- -

- -

- -

- -

. . .

WHO IS LUCY RUTH?

LUCY IS A MOTHER OF THREE, works fulltime and also runs an online business selling African heritage products. Her website is nhakayedu.com. Lucy was featured in a story by *The Weight She Carries* (weightshecarries.com) for her support of African artistry. The trajectory of her life changed at the age of ten when she lost her mother in her native, Zimbabwe. For years, Lucy struggled with depression and felt alone because depression was not a topic people discussed in Zimbabwe. This birthed a desire to connect with people.

Having lived and worked in three continents: Africa, Europe and now North America, Lucy has been exposed to different cultures and experiences. While customs vary, she has seen a common thread in every place she has lived; the challenges people face are the same. Gifted in being a good listener, Lucy is the voice of those who cannot stand up for themselves. She is passionate about equal opportunities for all and the empowerment of all people. In addition, Lucy has experience in airport operations, education in airline and travel and is a holder of 30 IATA points. She also has education in events management with public relations.

Facebook: https://m.facebook.com/LucyRuthofficial

Instagram: https://www.instagram.com/debunkdevelopyourmind/

LinkedIn: http://linkedin.com/in/lucy-r-b546113

Official website: https://www.lucyruth.page/

Email: info@lucyruth.page